INSPIRED BY THEIR SPIRITS

A Collection of Poems

Charles Portolano

INSPIRED BY THEIR SPIRITS
A Collection of Poems

by Charles Portolano

ProdCode: CSS/250/2.10/251/12

Library of Congress Catalog Card Number

99-076514

International Standard Book Number

1-55605-292-8

Printed in the United States of America

Wyndham Hall Press
Bristol, IN 46507-9460

We hope you enjoy our book.
Thank you for your support.

Sincerely,
[illegible signature]

For my wonderful wife Vivi,
my daring daughter Valerie Marie,
and all those families with children
with special needs,
thank you for the wings
so I could take flight...

Thank you Dr. Irwin Schwartz, Dr. Wesley Carrion, and, Dr. Michael Egnor for fighting to keep the integrity of our daughter Valerie Marie intact and for proving heroes still exist.

Thank you Grandma Simone Chiurazzi, Bernice Kornfield-Premisler, Rhona Goldman, and, Lucy Fleury for being our strong support team during our darkest days. You took care of all of us.

Thank you Mom and Dad Portolano for being such great parents and for always being there for us.

Thank you Elaine Belle, my all-time favorite teacher, for a ready eye to read my work and for all your kind words that kept me writing.

Thank you Dr. Morgan and Wyndham Hall Press for believing in my work.

PREFACE

No woman can make a man change, but a man's desire for a woman's love can make that man change for the better. The love a of good woman can make a boy forgo his boyish bravado. The first twelve poems of this collection reflect my transformation into a better human being. They tell of the love I always wanted in my life; for the rest of my life. Without that love I do not know if I would have been able to withstand the pain of the last four years. The next sixty poems tell of the events of the four years that followed.

My wife Vivi and I had ten wonderful years of martial bliss together. We would buy the house my wife grew up in. Two months later, we learned that Vivi was pregnant. The pregnancy proved to be very difficult. The outcome of the delivery was always in question. After the arduous delivery, I heard for the first time that Valerie should never have survived. I learned later that my wife's life was also in great jeopardy.

Two days after Valerie was born, she would take and fail an Otoacoustic Emissions hearing test. At two months old, she failed an Auditory Brainstem Response Test. Valerie was born with a bilateral hearing impairment. The roller coaster ride had begun. Vivi went through the five steps of grief much quicker than I. She had Valerie enrolled in the Early Intervention Program of New York State. Thank God we live in New York. Valerie had hearing aides, a speech teacher, a special education teacher, a physical therapist, and an occupational therapist before the age of three months. In hindsight the hearing loss was going to be the least of Valerie's problems. Valerie is living proof that Early Intervention works and will change the course of a child's life.

At thirteen months old, we ended up in the emergency room at 4:00 A.M. Valerie had a mysterious 105.8 degree temperature. A nuclear medicine scan confirmed Valerie had Pyelonephritis. 60-70% of her right kidney was permanently damaged. This is a rare diagnosis for a child so young. Red flags went up everywhere.

God was good. From the renal x-ray taken when Valerie was admitted for the Pyelonephritis, we learned that Valerie had a rare type of Congenital

Scoliosos, a L5 Hemivertebra. Dr. Schwartz, Valerie's Developmental Pediatrician, would assemble a world-class group of specialists to work with Valerie from the University Hospital at Stony Brook. Dr. Carrion, Pediatric Orthopaedic Surgeon, was called in to watch the progress of Valerie's spine. Dr. Carrion told my wife directly, "It is a miracle that Valerie was ever born."

On May 28, 1998, Dr. Carrion performed a Posterior Spinal Fusion. We were in the hospital for 39 days. Valerie had to be taught how to walk again. Valerie had severe post operative complications. Again, Valerie's survival was in serious question. If not for her Mother's ability to be proactive and such an assertive advocate, Valerie would not be with us today. I watched in horror the pain Valerie lived through. I watched in amazement how brave both of these woman were. I held my breath and held on for dear life. Valerie would start wearing a spinal brace for 23 hours out of each day. A period of calm came upon us.

In January of 1999, the storm returned. Valerie started complaining of severe headaches, intense neck pain, gagging, dizziness, and increased spinal pain. She stopped eating solid food, living on pediasure from the bottle to survive. The failure to thrive label reared its ugly head again. On June 23, 1999, Dr. Egnor, Pediatric Neurosurgeon, diagnosed Valerie with a rare type of Spina Bifida, Chiari malformation. In August, Vivi insisted surgery must be done. Dr. Egnor agreed. A Chiari Decompression surgery was performed on August 13, 1999. Eight stressful days later, Valerie shocked us all and walked out of the hospital whole. She still lives with pain, but her future and ours holds great promise.

Valerie's first four years have been mind-boggling. During that time, Valerie and Vivi displayed a rare heroic spirit. I watched in awe. Without that spirit we would not have overcome this difficult ordeal. From this experience, I grew spiritually as a man to become the man I always wanted to grow into. I thank God I was allowed to be a part of their extraordinary lives. I now walk with God and take nothing for granted.

Charles Portolano - 10/10/99

TABLE OF CONTENTS

THUNDERBOLT

So astonishing
from out of nowhere
struck by you from
way across the room
a bolt of warmth
out of the blue
stunning how
suddenly heated
lightning quick
I have grown
as our paths
flash together
I witness
the clashing clouds
confronting my
rising consciousness
with an eerie sense
of something special
about to occur as
your striking impact
awakens my heart
your magnetic force
pulls me near
rousing me
to find out
if the thundering
of your beauty
has the electrical
charge of love
lighting my horizon.

ELECTRIC

Within reach
without words
you speak
in streams
the mind
and spirit
of your heart
throbs a strong
signal through
trembling eyes
that dances
away the distance
between us
exciting these
dark eyes
to come alive
with a wave
of impulses
beating around
and around
to my heart
the warm rhythm
of your love so
I easily escape
into your arms
where the past
has no presence
for you are
the spark that
ignites my future.

ILLUMINATION

Aimlessly wandering
lost and lonely
in the thick wilderness
of my dark imagination
unable to envision
a way out for
the forces of fear
keep me captive
in my deep freeze
as my dark energies
drive me deeper
and deeper into
my frozen wasteland
lost in mediocrity
then your vision so
strong comes upon me
as your spirit visits me
spring boarding me to an
incredible metamorphosis
spellbinding me
to see far freer than
ever before unveiling
a festival to my eyes
a holiday for my heart as
your desire to guide me
with your unfailing light
allows me to escape
to a sense of sanity
for the wonder of your
love celebrates life.

COSMIC COUSINS

Understanding
one another
from first sight
we shoot out
of the void
straight into
orbit around
each other
where some
magical attraction
draws us together
blending our auras
as one we
trust fully
instantly revealing
our vulnerabilities
hidden from others
for so long now
order and harmony
drives our hearts'
deepest thoughts
as we travel
through the grand
vast areas
among the planets
and the stars
into the uncharted
space of pure
love forever
magnetized together.

THE MERRY-GO-ROUND

Seated on my high horse
I imagine I am
a cowboy riding
across the open plains
as I stretch myself
to grab the gold ring
slipping I miss
my chance this time
around realizing
life is a series
of circles knowing
I have something to
look forward to
as I ride around
and around I am
having the time
of my wild life
with all the daily
ups and downs I
enjoy the high spirit
of all the whirling
then you arrive
to ride next to me
so I stretch myself
reaching up knowing
this time I will not
miss my chance
to grab that gold ring
to give to you to be
my wonderful wife.

WAVELENGTH

Dancing where
the waves crash
daring the tide
to touch you
but the waves
lie down
at your feet
as your golden
skin soaks in
the warm rays
you stretch out
your young body
in the hot, sticky
white sand
breathing deep
under the staring
yellow sun
the waves undulate
across your view
as the tide
shyly kisses
your scarlet
red toenails
you lovingly laugh
having had
your way
with the waves
has heated up
the beach

now come home.

THE DANCING FLAME

The flickering flame
of the scented candle
gives off light
enough to guide
our way through
the darkness
we gaze on
one another
as the shy
orange-blue eye
silently watches
warming the room
our shadows start
to slow dance
far off into
the realm of touch
dancing as
we do arouses
the rising flame
slowly, surely
our flesh
melts in a blaze
of sweet desire
until the passion
becomes peace
dreaming of
one another
the flame
goes out
into the darkness.

YOU ALCHEMIST

Something about you
your art of knowing
changes the course
of my life
leading me from
my leaden ways
I transcend myself
through your spiritual
understanding I find
the hidden key
through your eyes
I clearly see
for the first time
a transformation
before my eyes
I watch your ways
with secret knowledge
of the unknown
waking my mind
sending me
far from here
where I can learn
to live in peace
to renew myself
for you are
impossible to resist
your riches
I want to hold
in my hands
as if gold.

AFFINITY

Traveling throughout
countless lifetimes
until the present
cosmic clock
aligns us together
in each other's arms
for we have entered
into an alliance
of our elite love
so fierce and strong
fusing our spirits
as a single body
of thought with
order and harmony
evolving our souls
to allow us
such freedom
from earthy wants
for with each kiss
a newness occurs
creating unflagging
bursts of pure energy
to lighten our load
of worldly worries
as our combined
forces promise
a future full of
exciting possibilities
to arrive at our
perfect place of peace.

BACKSTROKING

During my late
afternoon swim
while doing
the backstroke
your divine eyes
come to me
in powerful waves
as I stare
up to the heavens
the stillness
of the water
gives way to
my sweeping
motions propelling
me forward
with your image
shimmering inside
my head
I swim stronger
through this
body of water
free for all
is quiet beneath
the surface
except the sound
of your heartbeat
inspiring my every
stroke back to
you this sweet
summer night.

SPINE-TINGLING

To be as one
with you
to be in love
with you
living with you
waking to you
I feel you in
every cell
of my being
knowing your way
knowing your pain
I gain a sense
of my being
in your shoes
knowing you will
stand for me
frees me to feel safe
for your strength
you willingly share
cares for my every
waking moment
keeping me warm
long through
the dark night
when dreams tell me
being as one
with you is where
in the universe
I am meant to be
with you.

HAVING EVERYTHING

With such grace
you move
always on the move
through troubled
hard times
advocating your way
you carry yourself
with such daring
audacity always
making me dream
of dazzling days
alone together
those nights
so tender
always to be
remembered as
stolen moments
isolated from all
you caring for me
sharing with me
all your thoughts
etched deep within
wanted forever
as part of me
freeing me
to takeoff soaring
flying higher
seeing more than
I'd ever dreamed
ever dared thought.

BORN TO DANCE

From the moment
you could first move
you wriggled and
waggled your way
around inside
your Mother's womb
kicking up a storm
heating up our hearts
as we feel
your strong vibrations
of endless energy
flowing out to
our waiting fingers
you circle around
and around again
trembling forward
then backward
picking up the tempo
with wings on
your little feet
you swing wide
first this way then
back the other way
always buzzing
you quivering
with anticipation of
bursting out ready
to busy yourself on
the dance floor of life
we wait to applaud you.

THE COMING OUT

Arriving so early
sunnyside up
face to face
with love I was
love so new, you
so silent
for what did
seem forever
until you cried out
your protest
of being taken
from the sea
of tranquility
with your Mother
being braver than I
could ever be
bringing you out
like light
you arrive
coming upon us
love so new, you
allow us to be
more alive with
our fingertips
touching the heavens
as angels trumpet
your arrival, you
Valerie Marie
complete the sweet
circle of our lives.

KNOWING FOREVER

Propped up high
on my right elbow
I look down upon
how peacefully
Valerie lies across
your beautiful breasts
breathing so easy
her eyes closed
she sleeps content
as her long lashes
dance with life
her tiny arms
wrapped around you
she rides the wave
of your every breath
moving up and down
forever in love
with the sound
of our loving heart
I look to you
smiling so happy
for having made
such a special girl
who has proven to
be so very strong
having survived
her arduous journey
we know together
that we are looking
upon our future.

FREEDOM

Daring to make
brave new changes
to alter the course
of my life
taking charge
taking control
daring to rewrite
the deep-seated
imprinting found
on my mind
so I don't relive
or repeat the same
mistakes made
in the past as I
defy human nature
being proactive
deciding to break
those bad habits of
my boyish bravado
I lived through
so now I view life
as a challenge
making me
actively pursue
my focus
to find the way
to make you
proud of me
during our short
time we have here.

THE AWAKENING

The constant questions
coming at me
continuously make me
rethink everything
I thought I knew
for you make me
see a whole new
fresh vista
of the vast world
working your miracles
stirring me from
my deep sleep
of selfishness
opening my eyes
can't be myopic
for you make me
see beyond
my own horizon
rousing me to
the huge world
of responsibility
for I do worry
now that I am
consciously aware
for the first time of
what needs to be done
for you make me
rise above myself
through the sheer
power of your spirit.

THE BIG PICTURE

The constant stresses
of daily living
complicate everything
with so many pieces
of the puzzle
to pick from
leaving me confused
beyond bewildered
I attempt to find
quick answers
with easy solutions
to the many mysteries
that cause uncertainty
filling me with
an emptiness
about what to do
with my life
then you two
come to me
reach out to me
becoming part
of me instantly
I know of love
for you two are
allowing me to see
clearly the reason
for my existence
for you two are
all the pieces I'll
need to complete me.

ADVERSITY

Honoring no
boundaries
adverse winds
rip across
our blissful
landscape
challenging
the terrain
but the bond
between us
never wavers
ever ready
for the test
to weather
the assaulting
cold front
together we
adapt to
the unraveling
changing climate
overcoming
the test of time
we resonant
in our love
of each other
unbounded
by the risks
of living
when facing
misfortune.

THE SOURCE

I find spring
inside your soul
every time I see
our daughter
grow in laughter
knowing your caress
will protect her
from the grueling
grip of coldness
my heart sings
your praise
of the rhythm
of your warmth
that radiates
to all around
we catch your rays
of love as you
rejuvenate our faith
of a new beginning
from the cruel
cold world
that has forced
us into hiding
I find spring
in my spirit
and a bounce
in my step
every time I feel
your resilience
touch us.

THE PRINCESS

I sit in awe of you,
Valerie Marie,
my precious daughter
on this grand day
your proud Mother
queenly parades you
around for all
the well-wishers
to see you
adorn each with
that divine stare
of sovereign
blue eyes in
porcelain white skin
with feet that
never touch
the floor
you float from
room to room
your regal way
reigns sunshine
to all you grace
on this day
more a coronation
that a fist birthday
celebration of
your being
heir-apparent
for princess
of the planet.

OUR SOLIDARITY

How fitting we are
always together
holding tight
against the rush
of worldly worries
that whirl
our way
through the dark
anxieties of life
that compound
our need
to lean on
each other
for the chemistry
between us
has bonded
our love forever
so with each test
we grow stronger
understanding now
that the constant
build up of pressure
from all directions
makes us hold
that much tighter
as if we were joined
at the elbows ready
to withstand all
of the worries
that come each day.

OUR SATURDAY DATES

You are you
survivor
living through far
more in your few
years than most
in a lifetime
I admire you
your strength
so young
so brave
straight-shooting
graceful in what
you want
you communicate
so clearly you speak
more and more
so sure of yourself
I always feel proud
in McDonalds
on Saturdays
when you laugh
riding the horses
jumping and playing
with the children
laughing loud like
I know I do when
having fun like this
I thank God
you are you and
we have Mommy.

OUR HURRICANE

Early in the morning
you reduce your room
to ruin tossing
your blankets and
pillows off your bed
as you reel
around and around
growing giddy
by the moment
you shatter the silence
with your laughter
thundering throughout
the peaceful house
you wreak havoc
on everything
found in your path
leaving the den
in a state
of devastation
with all your toys
scattered everywhere
you storm
into our bedroom
dizzy with excitement
whirling around and
around us so we
are forced to rush
from our warm bed
out of fear for
the safety of our home.

THE PRINCESS AT TWO

So powerful in personality
you have grown
these two years
as you parade
around this planet
you are always a royal
good time
for you are
a divine gift
from God
with your Mother's smile
her bold blue eyes
and sensibilities
you make us
better human beings
for we have grown from
your having traveled
such a great distance
in your short existence
filling our dreams
with laughter
and our hearts
with love for you
Princess Valerie Marie
are so much
like your Mother
how lucky a man
I am to be
surrounded by you two.

THE DRIVING FORCE

You are everything
in her eyes
looming larger
that life
in the early days
of her existence
when she waits
on your every
warm word
and the kindness
of your touch
means so much
for her to grow
healthy and wise
to the ways
of this world
where one wrong
turn can lead her
down a dead end
of no return
so she looks up
to you to give
her direction
to steer clear
and maneuver
around all
the roadblocks of
living to arrive
at the truth
of her future.

THE ORDEAL

Not knowing
what to expect
when the natural
order of things
becomes out of sync
we are powerless
to control
what happens next
so we need to be
guided by our faith
not our fears
never letting worries
overwhelm us
as we use the pain
to power our purpose
forcing our focus
to become fearless
facing life's trails
we become the
advocates in charge
of what must be
done as we learn
from this experience
what is important
what is necessary
on how to exist
with so much less
to not only survive
but to come away
knowing courage.

THE TAINTED ONES

Riding high on the wave
of the American dream
so dizzy in our pursuit
of happiness
with everything
we could ever want...

Then one day
without warning
a sudden turn
of events comes
crashing down
upon our world and
everything we knew
doesn't look, feel
or seem the same
as yesterday
before this dark
cloud of gloom
surrounded us
with the unthinkable
making our nightmare
world our reality
as everyone that we
thought we knew
now avoids us
in our time of need
out of fear
that what has
befallen us might
plague their world.

UNIFIED FRONT

Instantly attracted
to the timelessness
of the ever moving
power of our love
together carries us
through this life
as we share
all the idyllic
dreamlike moments
and those dark days
when difficult decisions
must be made
for events do go
beyond our control
so we fight for the light
mirroring the mettle
that we are made of
deep inside
gathering the strength
to bounce back
responding as one
positive force
proactive in action
dealing with purpose
to bring about
the desired result
that truly reflects
the wonderful trust
we feel for each other.

WAITING FOR SUNSHINE

Waiting takes its terrible
toll on the imagination
not knowing what to
expect next as time ever
so slowly ticks away
I struggle with myself
for the spiritual strength
to remain strong
rocking in this chair
staring at the ceiling
pulling my hand
through my tangled hair
unaware of the world
lost in limbo
without light
waiting on this wall
of darkness blackening
my thoughts to be
lifted so this assault
on my nervous system
can cease as I wait
for you to open your
wonderful blue eyes
to hear your sweet
voice whisper my name
to be warm again
seeing your smile
shining out to us
so we can all once
again do our sun dance.

AT THE CROSSROADS

There are those few
defining moments
in my life
that give direction
to my future
forcing me to face
my own reality
searching my soul
gathering the strength
to resist temptations
to turn down
the low road where
I run the risk
of making inroads
into the shadows
of alibis
that steer me
to the easy way out
or do I hold tight
to my mettle
driven by some
hidden insight
that the road ahead
will be rough
discovering just how
strong I must be
taking the high road
to make it through
the difficult choices
of one's life.

SHATTERED

Rocked to the core
of my very being
as the tears
well up in my eyes
watching you
withering in pain
a coldness clouds
my thinking
leaving me no
place to hide
knowing I am
unable to soothe you
or secure you
any peace
I stand emptied
of all my strength
as the shadow
of fear grips me
purging me
of any bravado
chaos comes swirling
making me weak
in the knees
I grab the bed railing
holding on
for dear life
praying all this
will disappear
I squeeze your hand
to hold back my tears.

MIND-BOGGLING

Squeezing strength
into my hand
straight to my heart
races with pride
my eyes come alive
seeing you rise up
from the ashes
I watch you spring
back with amazement
wondering how
always at the moment
of truth you are
so resilient
adapting to every
new strange situation
thrown at you
transcend yourself
always following
your inner instincts
maneuvering around
all the roadblocks
with remarkable grace
for someone so young
you have a sixth sense
of yourself that so
few will ever know
allowing me some
semblance of peace
wanting to believe
this too shall pass.

THE FIRING LINE

The weight seems
so overwhelming
just too much
going on all the time
for my own good
coming too fast
can't be processed
all at one time
nearing overload
living on adrenaline
for far too long
with the senses
working overtime
without a rest
draining me of
all my energy
got to watch out
red flag everywhere
going to come
crashing down soon
so I must hold on
too many people
depending on me
to stay cool
on top of things
for now is the time
to see what I am
really made of
so I can finally
define myself.

RECOVERING

Shut down for so
long waiting
for you to finally
overcome the pain
to walk again
taking those first
few steps when
the fear disappears
you chance being
weight-bearing again
I hold my breath
as you dare attempt
those first few
toe touches
I hold on to you
making sure my grip
won't slip
consumed with fear
that you might
fall to the floor
but you move
through to your
first steps unaided
glad to be out
of that small room
knowing you'll be
soon screaming
for me to chase
you down these halls
to come catch you.

THE HOMECOMING

The long siege
has suddenly stopped
bringing peace
from the many battles
that have been waged
the war is over
we can go home
back to our quiet lives
as it was before
this difficult ordeal
never to forget
when the fighting
grew feverish
fear overcame me
not letting me think
if I would ever
see you again
standing tall
surviving the onslaught
of those dark nights
then the dawn
finds you smiling
adapting to all adversity
always smiling
warming everyone
around you so
the war is over
the many battles fought
have been survived
to come home whole.

ALIGHTING MY LIFE

Inspired by your
death-defying spirit
taking flight
when you walked
out whole from
that hospital
leaving a deep
indelible imprint
forever on
my consciousness
forcing me to
transcend myself
finding my way
to overcome
my weakness to
become the man
I've always wanted
with an awareness
of life's absurdity
making me see
how to handle
the challenges
of chasing away
those dark shadows
that cloud one's
view of your sweet
smile that guides me
to a smooth landing
into my long awaited
anticipated happiness.

FLASH-POINT

Bursting back into
your old being
taking those great
leaps and bounds
each day step by step
you stretch yourself
strong-willing your
way into the hearts
and imaginations of
everyone watching
you zeroing in
on the essence
of your situation
with that certain
savior-faire always
charming all around
you blaze into
strange, new territory
while enduring
your never-ending
existence of pain
you grow again
into your old self
smiling and laughing
understanding as you
regenerate yourself
right before our eyes
your spirit ignites
taking the world
by surprise.

BACK ON TRACK

Everything changed
when the darkness
came and the war
had to be won
now you play
catch-up so fast
you make us
dizzy laughing
dashing all day
as if there were
no tomorrow
amazing everyone
with the way you
always carry on
being daring doing
something new
every second
your eyes are open
so aware of what
is within you
regain your balance
never trading down
those dreams that
now cascade
in your young mind
as you drink in
the elixir of love
determined to be
ready to run
the race to win.

THE SUN DANCE

We can focus again
on the fun of living
now that the long
reign of darkness
is over your pain
has been purged
freeing you from
your confinement
to stargaze
at the heavens
rigorously renewing
your great urge to
explore your world
finds you waiting
in the green garden
for the tomatoes
to turn red
only to run out
testing the limits
you take flight
dashing straight for
the dangerous street
laughing when caught
we circle around
and around
together daring
to dance again
frolicking in overdrive
under the smiling sun
growing so strong.

TOUR-DE-FORCE

To step out of
the shadow world
passing from one place
to the next
always on the move
undertaking such
an expedition
over rough terrain
so early in life
you keep marching on
in war and peace
always energized
in constant motion
out to discover
secrets to be revealed
you keep marching on
stronger, longer
each new day
leaving the troubled
shaky start behind
you keep traversing
your universe
in search of what
is important
learning to bend
without breaking
in your force
of existence
you answer
all of our prays.

VALERIE MARIE AT THREE

Always on the upswing
from our lost summer
surprisingly surpassing
all my expectations
for you truly are
the splendor
of my happy dreams
as you sleep soundly
I stand over you
smiling knowing
you are now safe
wanting to believe
those dark days
are far behind us
as you challenge
my authority with
such unbelievable
freshness every day
you command respect
for I must consider
what I say and do
to make sure you
grow into the person
that your potential
has planned for you
display rare courage
I could never have
dreamed that I'd
be blessed with such
a daring daughter.

STOLEN MOMENTS

A sudden springtime
freshness returns
as if we were
young lovers again
holding hands
stealing away
into the night
to a secluded spot
where no one
will find us
we rejoice in
our lost moments
when first we
kissed and touched
each other's hearts
exploring these golden
minutes alone
with you looking
so young in the glow
of the white candles
dancing in the dark
you whisper my name
ever so softly
at this moment
I know the greatness
of our love
has grown
each passing year
with the arrival
of our dear daughter.

MY CD PLAYER

She has waited
all day for me
to come home
to turn her on
bringing her to life
with a touch
she plays whatever
my mood is
if angry
she plays loud
if I am sad
she will turn sad
but when I am happy
she spins
out of control
around and around
doing anything
to make me smile
and make me want
to listen to her
for she has waited
all day for me
to bring her to life
to play the music
I have put inside
so she can spin
out of control
around and around
bringing happiness
to my dancing heart.

GUARDIAN ANGEL

From her first breath
you watch over her
bonding with her
always working
to bring her peace
in an angry world
you wait to catch her
if she might fall
you are her safety net
against all ill will
night and day
always smiling on her
always on the alert
you look in while
she is sleeping
so she knows
she can trust you
to be there for her
with that twinkle
in your blue eyes
you are looking
over her shoulder
ready to help lift her
in tough times
you take so much
pressure off her
so she can catch
her breath again
for you are always
watching over her.

THE GARDEN

A sigh of relief quickly
flows from you
the moment you enter
its wonderful aura
reaches out to you
drawing you in
to protect you
saving your sanity
digging deep
into that hard ground
preparing to raise crops
you have great fun
in the open air
getting out
all that anger
laying out the beds
is good therapy
turning over that earth
getting exercise
working off the stress
hanging loose
with the vegetables
waiting for your touch
knowing each day
you will care for them
cultivating a place
of peace with you
watching over them
growing so straight
under the summer sun.

THE ROLLER-COASTER

Climbing the steep incline
inching my way
to the top
then that quick
descent rushes
all that adrenaline
rushes my fingers
to grip that bar
for the first time
holding tighter
as I go so fast
down that my heart
leaves me losing
my breath behind me
then slowly I
loosen my grip as
thing level out
I gain momentum
coming into
that tight turn wide
nearly veering
out of control
I hold on for dear life
with my heart
wildly in love
with the adrenaline
I dare all dashing
into the next thrill
learning to enjoy
the ride of my life.

IN ANOTHER'S SHOES

If I could jump
right out of my skin
into the shoes
of another
to suddenly experience
the feelings
of another
whole new world
through a completely
different perspective
to learn of another's
loves and hates
to know their fears
live with their doubts
their concerns
feel their pain
I would learn to be
not so quick
to judge others
as I walk
in their footsteps
down a different path
I gain insight into
a new way of being
making me grow
with the power
to appreciate
how much alike
we all really are
under the skin.

MOUNTAIN-CLIMBING

Into the valley
of dreams
we are born
to struggle up
the slippery slopes
to stumble
in the dark
off the path
where our hearts
haunt us
we tumble
down the incline
into the depression
lost in inactions...

Then one day
one's heart is drawn
in by the lure
of adventure
to take off
with flights
of fancy
through to the
glorious moments
of discovery
that one's
viselike grip is
always scaling
up to the summit
in the pursuit
of your truth.

THE LIGHT

Hearty your old soul
in a state of grace
being highly evolved
you warm all
of us around you
with your wisdom
for your silent intensity
constantly confronts
our anger turning
that negative charged
energy positive
bringing about a
change of heart
while you shoulder
our burden you
allow us who
should walk
in your shadow
to take your hand
guiding us to
an understanding
to free ourselves
by finding a focus
a true purpose for
our existence
knowing now that
people are what is
important if we are
to ever have happiness
while on this planet.

REFUELING

Even for this short time
being between battles
far off the front lines
away from the warfare
rest does not come easy
and to relax is near
impossible for it
seems a lifetime ago
not to have to hear
the constant sound
of discord exploding
all around us
so now we rendezvous
in secret to learn
how to breathe again
in each other's arm
getting much needed
recharging of spirits
for this downtime
with you my love
provides a refreshing
source of sustenance
for me to exist on
to carry out my duty
that must be done
knowing our time
together will be short
before we must
force ourselves to
face our worst fears.

THE CONUNDRUM

Having experienced
a near death event
I now see the light
electrifying my chances
to change the course
that my life was
leading me to
finally take control
of my emotions
learning how to forgive
for the first time
to truly be in love
with my life so
I transcend time
totally unafraid
of the darkness
while struggling to
know how to purge
myself of anger
that keeps my energy
from flowing freely
to bridge the gap
between my physical
and spiritual existence
so I can tap into
the wellspring deep
within my soul
bringing my spirit
to the surface
to soar free for infinity.

FORBIDDEN ZONE

An irresistible desire
indulges your
insatiable curiosity
to venture off
going where you
know you should not
you dare anyway
seeking a sense
of independence
you separate from us
with a new awareness
of who you are
for fear is overrun by
a restless imagination
as you tiptoe down
that long hallway
slowly opening the door
to go undetected
but the sudden silence
sounds our alarms
so we sneak up
to catch you in the act
for your little laugh
allows us to know
you are up to no good
doing something you
know you should not
stand there with
red lipstick all over
your triumphant face.

OUR DANDELION

Favored by us for
your steadfast mindset
to survive under
difficult conditions
you little yellow flower
so sweet on the surface
wild of heart
one with nature
time-tested tough
with no failure
to thrive here
sprouting out
wherever you can
growing free
under the caring sun so
I grow to admire
your willingness
to do whatever
you put your mind
to never take no for
the only answer as
you do what you will
always telling me no
you sprout up right
before my very eyes
with that warm smile
that lion's bite
behind it all
daring to laugh in
the face of adversity.

DANCE OF AN ANGEL

Your brilliant spirit's
enthusiasm for life
is so apparent as
your agile young body
dances deliriously
to the upbeat music
that you requested
I put on for you
move with such grace
soaring in
your unique way
for some inner drive
allows you to go
way beyond dizzy
around and around
keeping your big eyes
on me to see if
I am watching how
smoothly you glide
across the living room
coming perfectly out
of your pirouette
with warm open arms
to place a sweet kiss
on your Daddy's lips
as you step back
spinning around me
leaving me laughing
thinking how I love
my little ballerina.

IN THE BEGINNING

Her many bouts
with sickness
have made you both
inseparable
lives intermingled
more intimate
than most for
with each illness
you revolve around
each other
towards a stability
a sense of peace
as the earth
moves around
the warming sun
you wake to
each other
going to sleep
knowing the other
is always there
so fear never enters
as a constant for
you will be together
through the years
time will tell
of your love
growing stronger
as did once
a cold, new planet
around a young sun.

HELPLESS

As you cry yourself
to sleep each night
silently sobbing
I shudder knowing
I can bring you
no solace or relief
as my stoic stance
crumbles I
collapse to my knees
searching the heavens
begging please for
an answer to help
keep my head up
for my fears
must be faced
no fleeing from
reality now nor
dismissing the horror
I feel when I am
unable to protect you
knowing I must
reconcile myself
to remain brave
is all I can do
to keep from being
immobilized by this
deeply disturbing
turn of events
that brings darkness
to our broken hearts.

JUGGERNAUT

When the bad news
grew worse
becoming unbearable
making breathing
almost impossible
there is no way
we could ever stop to
think how hard life is
or to get off the path
just keep putting
our best foot forward
taking the days as
they come flying by
for events are too far
beyond our control
so all we could do
is keep running
as fast as we can
praying and hoping
not to be crushed
by the staggering
realization that this
is to be our fate
forever running
trying to stay
one step ahead
of the unrelenting
rush of worries
wanting to roll-over
our sensibilities.

LIVING IN LIMBO

Waiting on the unwanted
takes its toll
on my patience
for there is no denying
that this must be done
as my heartbeat
pounds against
my tightening chest
the thunderous ticking
of the cruel clock
leaves me with no
distraction from the pain
for life is upended
suspended for now
I am disconnected
from the everyday
having too much time
on my hands
ties up my thoughts
keeping me a prisoner
contemplating the worst
for that ticking
is pure torment
preventing me from
ever being proactive
I am straight-jacketed
unable to fight
the magnifying effect
of just waiting
for something to happen.

THE TOUCHSTONE

Searching the heavens
for earthy answers to
unravel the mysteries
of why adversity
is the only pathway
for us to evolve
to a higher level
of being for we
seem so indifferent
unable to understand
compassion and empathy
that is buried deep
in our human spirit
unless we ourselves
have survived moments
of great difficulty
running the gauntlet
that test our ability
to grasp reality
by tuning into
our natural instincts
so we can turn
away from hate
forcing us to come
through the darkness
to finally arrive
at enlightenment
to accept that we
must learn to
suffer to become pure.

THE OUTSIDERS

Treating us as if
we were tainted
drastically different
not to be talked to
for there is this
dark cloud over us
making all hide
when they see us
they run away
deeply afraid
we might affect
their quiet lives
bringing them down
they dare not have
any contact with us
being untouchable
our self-righteous
society ostracizes us
so unconcerned
about trampling
over our feelings
they look through us
making us invisible
as their coldness
becomes cruelty
causing great pain
we learn to stand
alone to survive
this sad perception
that is our reality.

OUT ON A WALKABOUT

My unrelenting fears
wake me to the dawn
for my grief grows
so great in the night
I can barely breathe
as my thinking
overwhelms me
I am dragged down
by my demons
who won't let
my heart be heard
so I start to walk
alone with tears
streaming down
my burning cheeks
raw with redness
I aimlessly walk
numb with despair
hoping to heal
my heavy heart
I walk all day
stopping to stare
into the setting sun
fills me with wonder
for the light is life
as I grow so tired
returning home now
emotionally ready to
finally collapse into
the coming darkness.

COURAGE

To stand strong
never cower
with enough nerve
so my shoulders
never sag even
though the weight
of the pain
is great as
my heart pounds
against my chest
when forced to face
the crucible
of life's most
terrible moments
I must muster
all my strength
during these darkest
days and defy
the urge to waver
under the pressure
withstanding and
enduring the ever
growing danger
with a true heart
that ventures out
to overcome
all the odds
all those fears
with a defiance
to persevere.

COLD-HEARTED

How cruel you were
carrying on
about the new house
overlooking the city
where you stroll
down the avenues
Sunday mornings
with your young wife
and healthy daughter
to have breakfast
and stop to shop
buying a new toy
or a trinket
to make your girls
swoon over your
great generosity for
you proudly show off
to the whole world
how well you are
doing now that
you made it big
so wrapped up
with yourself
you forget to think
about your words
being daggers into
my dark heart
over the hard facts
I have to face
every day of my life.

THE TRIGGER

When we ended up here
you grew silent
ever so tense
as sadness
suddenly surfaces
across your face
you withdraw
into yourself
filling the car
with a blackness
too thick to pretend
it does not exist
for we both know you
will have nightmares
for nights to come
even weeks
reliving the memories
you desperately
try to block out
instead they haunt you
never letting you rest
they drain you of life
leaving you questioning
your actions
your instincts
remembering the events
that changed you
with me knowing now
that we will never be
passing this way again.

RETREATING

Suffering silently
watching the rising
and falling
of your chest
I fall back
to another time
when all was
innocent and easy
walking along
that quiet road
hand in hand
waiting on
the setting sun
so we could kiss
without a care
then withdraw
from the road
down a dirt path
secluded from sight
we make our way
to where the wild
river runs free
rushing forward
we put our feet
in the cool water
laughing as only
the young do when
new to the senses
a spiritual renewal
allowing me to sleep.

THE DREAM

From out of nowhere
the turbulence hits us
thunder and lightning
raining hard
wave after wave
crashing over us
dashing all our hope
as we are thrown
completely off kilter
for this ship is
springing leaks
taking on water
as ruthless winds
slit through the sails
the mast comes
smashing down
fear of being dragged
under into the deep
darkness surfaces
knowing no shoreline
to swim to safety
nor will the lifeboats
ever preserve us
chaos takes over
all order is lost
putting us far off
our set course
we got to hold on
riding this one out
is all we can do.

IN THE DARK

In your peaceful arms
in the middle of
this dark night
I can almost forget
what the future
demands we face
for now it is warm
and quiet here
under these covers
I can feel free
from feeding my fears
if only for a while
hearing your heartbeat
watching you sleep
makes me wish
we could disappear
into the night
as I foolishly dream
of a way to stop
the advancing dawn
bringing down upon us
our daunting duty
that must be done
for there is no
escaping the inevitable
so now I will just
hold on to you
praying I have
the strength to make
you proud of me.

LIVING HELL

Handing her over
to the doctors
to care for
trusting them
with my love
while I wait
in a small room
far down the hall
for countless hours
I am helpless
unable to sit still or
make small talk
pounding hard
my white knuckles
against the wall
trying to forget
how long she cried
when they came
to get her
digging her nails
into my hands
as they wheeled
her away I could
only walk behind
praying she would
understand that we
had no choice
if she was ever to
know any peace
while on earth.

THE LIGHTHOUSE

Dignity in adversity
standing tall in
rain, sleet, hail
you weather
all the storms
shining brightly
even when the sun
runs from the darkness
you dare stare
straight out for all
to see your beacon
sending out warnings
serving all in need
you reach out
to those lost
giving guidance
draws me to you
for I am far off course
in dangerous waters
I know you will
show me to safety
never leaving me
I dream of being
the terra firma
beneath your feet
connected to you
together we tower
against gravity with
me living in the light
of your warm love.

FINDING YOUR VOICE

Now nearing four
A twist of fate again
Forces you to become
A statistic
Bringing you back into
This hostile environment
Compromising you
Your future
Forcing you to fight against
These hard facts
As we all relive our worst fears
Waiting for you to wake
Is endless
Faith be with us
You emerge from the long darkness
Come see, you say
Blinking both of your blue eyes
Your sparkle dull, lifeless
You whisper not a word
Opening and closing
Your little right hand
Waving hello
To signal your return...

Your wounded head hasn't moved
For three full days
From that bloodstained pillow
As we watch
Worrying over you
Still your will shines through
The sparkle can be seen again
Working through
The paralyzing pain
Come see, you say
Weaning yourself off
The powerful morphine
With not a crack

In your porcelain china
You whisper:
"A little water, please"
Your voice weakened
From the cutting-edge
Brain surgery
You have survived
With both Grandmothers watching
Worrying over you
They guard against germs
Wanting to keep you safe...

Slowly you work up the courage
To move your head side to side
Come see, you say
Moving your head again and
Again-side to side
Finally you summon
All your strength
Working through the pain
Working through the fear
You prop up your shaky head
Held high
Cupped in your right hand
Supported on you right elbow
Are the first signs
Of progress
Allowing us a moment
To breathe again
As you tell us:
"I don't like hospitals.
They are mean places.
When can we go home?"
And then you raspberry me
So we know you are
On your way back to us...

Knowing what has to be done
If you are to leave
You work all day
Rolling and wiggling around
In your small hospital bed
Surrounded by your stuffed dog Dino
And countless Barbie dolls
You eat more than ever
Getting bossier
By the moment
We know it is only
A matter of time
Before you make your move
Bouncing back
Come see, you say
As you wind your way
Right up into
A sitting position
Smiling:
"I knew I could do it.
I knew I would sit-up again..."

We are amazed
Our eight-day stay is over
We are leaving
Walking out the elevator
We hold both your hands
Through the lobby
Laughing for we are leaving
Suddenly you break free
Come see, you say
Walking out the automatic doors
Walking outside on your own
You spin around and around
Under the blue August sky
Your very own little person
You return back to us
With the sparkle glowing
In your beautiful, blue eyes

And that smile of yours
Hinting of the dickens again
You find your voice:
"I knew I would get out.
I knew I would not be there long."

FOUR AND MORE TO COME

You are four and
now I know
there will be more
years to come
for you have survived
being alive
thrills me to
see your will
shine through
all the darkness
that descended upon
you still smile
while the pain
remains with you
you grow stronger
after your ordeal
I feel safe
to say you are
special something
in your eyes shows
the ties that bond us
together forever
I will be in awe
of you, my daughter
Valerie Marie
now that you have
reached the golden
age of four
Happy Birthday
many more to come.

WARM THOUGHTS

With all decisions made
you should draw
a line in the sand
knowing just how far
you are willing to go
can only come
from being brought up
knowing love
where limits
are made and
accommodations exist
to be explored
to learn from
for in the near future
you will need to know
that one must stand
on your own
in this cruel world
that demands
decisions be made
by the minute
you must be ready
if need be
to tiptoe that line
steady as you go
making your way
by remembering
all those long walks
on the beach
with your proud Mother.

completion of your climb.
only up to see the
to never look down
as you reach an understanding
tight your grip onto each rung
around you forcing you to hold so
the clouds with the wind blowing
this never ending ladder into
your destiny to climb up
for you to have faith in
you get to a sense of self
so with each step the closer
you might let go of your hold
climb for if you were to stop
of regret, you just climb and
you take with no thought
next step, each step you take
not knowing what pushes your
as your confidence grows
for life is looking up
one way up, no looking down
you won't stop for there's only
to the top, to the top
trust blind faith, you continue
in a world where you must
the closer you get to the top
with each step, each step
you could even crawl
up this ladder began before
This climb, this climb

UPLIFTING